INSIGHTS

NAVIGATING THE FIRST 100 DAYS

[handwritten inscription]

ILLUSTRATED BY LAURA CARLIN

Taylor Bennett

FOREWORD

In partnership with our wide network of senior and influential communications professionals, we have great pleasure in presenting this special 30th-anniversary book to share tips, insights and anecdotes on how best to navigate the crucial early stages of a new job.

While there is a wealth of information and experience to draw on from within these pages, it seems clear that the first 100 days will be a lot easier if you listen hard, be yourself, trust your instincts and work the shoe leather. Gaining a deep cultural understanding of your new organisation is seen as one of the most important considerations – those most likely to succeed know how to network internally and externally. Equally, the ability to retain an objective perspective is a critical element of long-term integrity. As one contributor says, "Bring in the fresh air; bring in the voice of reality; be the voice of the outside world; mean what you say; be authentic." As you would probably expect, there are differences of opinion within the book and diverse points of view. No one size fits all, it would seem, and certain suggestions will work best in certain situations. The smart individual will be prepared for any scenario or corporate culture and we hope that this smorgasbord of collected experience will better equip the new starter.

You will see that not everyone who has contributed had the luxury of time when they joined their new organisation; the financial crisis put quite a few people under the spotlight immediately, for example. Many feel that arriving in a crisis can have advantages, when adrenalin and professionalism

Whilst the main chapters of this book consist of direct quotes from senior communications practitioners, the 'Overarching view' sections reflect a single-voice perspective: a different person for each chapter.

kick in, with instant access to key stakeholders and the opportunity to make a fundamental difference to an organisation's reputation. Whenever you join, being seen to be effective, influential and confident will go a long way to building your credibility – and that of your team.

Team leadership, for most people in senior positions, plays a major part of any role. In today's demanding world, where individuals expect more management time and have greater expectations for active career development, understanding your own skills as an authentic, committed and enabling leader will be important. Before starting a new job, many stress the value in taking some time to reflect on your own style, working practices and past successes. What approach will you take, what type of capabilities will you look for, and how will you manage your own profile and reputation internally?

And the view from the top? When taking a brief, we ask our clients a very simple question: "What will success look like?" In the words of one of our FTSE CEO clients, "Success to me is hiring someone who can create simple, clear, consistent, repeatable and repeated messages. I need a storyteller." It seems that doing the simple things well will not only go a long way in your first 100 days, but throughout your career.

This practical guide, therefore, is structured across the traditional first 100-day timeframe and covers topics such as internal politics, the value of networking, team leadership and strategy setting. We hope that it both amuses and informs.

The contributors have been most generous with their time and their willingness to share their experience, for which we thank them most sincerely.

WHAT WE SAY ABOUT OURSELVES

Taylor Bennett is a global executive search firm specialising in finding and placing senior and mid-level corporate communications professionals. We offer specialist experience across the corporate, public and not-for-profit sectors and also in core disciplines such as investor relations, internal communications, public affairs, media relations and marketing communications.

WHAT OTHERS
SAY ABOUT US

"Taylor Bennett is the established leader in its field as communications headhunters. In my dealings with them, from both the public and private sectors, they add exceptional value because they know the market and players exceptionally well – and throughout the appointment process are scrupulous in keeping lines of communication open. They have impeccable judgement and are a delight to deal with."

"They really get to know their candidates. They are tough and realistic about who can thrive in what circumstances. At its heart, that is about going the extra mile to find the right person with good prospects of a lasting fit."

"Taylor Bennett did a first-class job for me. Their knowledge, understanding and quick, seamless service meant that it was a very positive experience working with them."

"The quality of support you get from TB is the best I've come across and always has been."

www.taylorbennett.com
+44 (0)20 7580 4300

CONTENTS

BEFORE YOU JOIN

"I WISHED I HAD
TAKEN SOME TIME
BEFORE STARTING
MY NEW JOB.
I WAS SHATTERED
FROM MY OLD JOB."

From Taylor Bennett's perspective, it goes without saying that even before considering a new role it makes sense to be sure about simple things such as the reporting line, job spec, team dynamics, expectations, and the mandate itself. However, we are realistic about the fact that you might not always have the benefit of a good headhunter to help you, so flag that your own success in navigating those first 100 days could depend heavily on the work done before joining.

→ Be prepared to have your bubble burst. All the excitement of a new job can evaporate when the security guard thinks that as the 'communications adviser', you have come to fix the phones.

→ **Read the job spec, and then find out what's *not* included. Even then, that little line about an 'occasional requirement to serve as chief of staff' might come back to haunt you...**

Don't lose heart. In the first three months you will probably uncover all sorts of problems and issues. This is quite normal.

→ Your first 100 days begin the day you are appointed. Start immediately to understand the environment and the issues you are going to be taking on. Even while wrapping up my old job, I came in and met people so that when I did actually arrive, I already had a good idea of what needed to be done. These were one-on-one as well as group meetings, across the organisation. I was brought in with a very clear mandate to make changes.

→ If you are going into a totally new sector, you can feel like an alien. I would recommend research into the company culture – and the CEO's expectations. What does success look like for him? My job had been newly created and I was regarded with some suspicion and felt susceptible to political sabotage. Never underestimate how vulnerable people might feel when you join the organisation. You will need to be robust and prepared.

→ Get meetings in the diary with regional partners before you arrive, especially if you are working with leadership – they can be out of touch with the rest of the business. I had to reassess my plans and strategy because I only met the leadership team at regional offices after four months in the job, and they had important feedback and different perspectives. I could have done with building up my knowledge of the corporate history more quickly, too.

→ Beware of bad timing when moving jobs. I was made redundant once before I even started the job because of unexpected year-end budget slashes by the parent company.

→ **Be prepared for the unexpected. You may have the best-laid plans for your first 100 days but, as happened to me, the CEO might take you into his confidence on day one and talk about an imminent takeover or significant strategic change in direction.**

"THE WORST
MISTAKE IS TO
TRASH WHAT
OTHER PEOPLE
HAVE DONE
BEFORE."

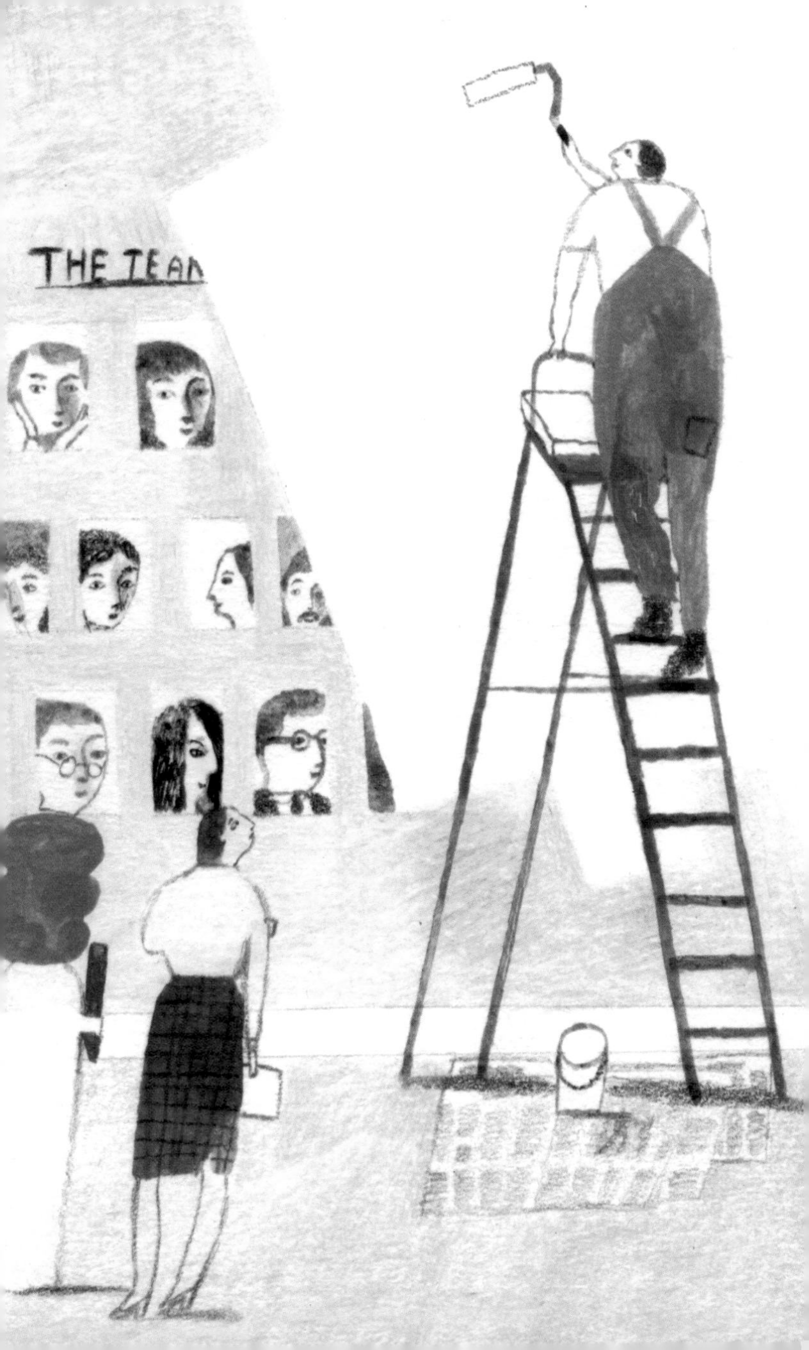
THE TEA

There is the job description and then there is the job; navigate the reality of the situation. You will arrive in a very territorial world and will need to be a diplomat while at the same time demonstrating discipline and being clear about what you expect from people.

Make sure there is some sort of induction programme.

My most memorable first 100 days involved travelling to the New York HQ of the company I'd just joined for a 'getting to know you' session, only to be asked for my advice on how to handle the imminent sacking of the guy back in London who had just hired me. Happily I went on to have a long and rewarding job with the company in question, but it was a stark reminder that corporate culture isn't always what it looks like from the outside.

I wish I had taken more time off before starting. I was shattered from my previous job.

Moving from a long career in journalism into communications posed some interesting challenges. Half the newsroom decided they instantly had a direct line into my new (very high-profile) boss. Our media line was swamped with requests, all mentioning me. The other half filled my inbox with their CVs, seeking jobs. Some hedged their bets and pitched for an interview and a new job in the same email. My advice? If you're making a similar move, try to lower expectations before leaving your old employer.

Be careful about checking the job spec against your contract – the titles might not always line up...

Everything you do tends to be massively over-amplified before you join. For example, an innocent comment during an on-boarding coffee meeting was interpreted as criticism. It is very difficult to guard against this, but try to be sensitive right from the first coffee.

On my first day I was really impressed that the CEO, despite being on holiday himself at the time, had left a hand-written note on my desk to welcome me. It was a simple but highly effective touch and one that could be duplicated with one's own team. It felt as if I was wanted and my arrival was anticipated with pleasure.

I wish I had asked my CEO more specifically what he thought success would look like for my role and pushed him harder on his genuine commitment to communications.

It turned out that there were tensions in my new team because people had wanted my job and been passed over. It would have been helpful to know this.

"GET ROUND YOUR CLIENTS – HEAR THEIR HONEST VIEWS."

It is very easy to go in to a new role in a new organisation and think, 'I need to ease my way in gently'. That is wrong. Start the way you mean to go on and don't appear too cautious.

Communications is a function that consistently needs to earn its place at the top table. As a leader, you have to be the exemplar for strategic counsel. Don't freak out that you don't know everyone and everything that's going on. As a senior adviser and with your professional background and skills, you have the right to ask probing questions. The objectivity of ignorance can be a hugely valuable thing, but you only get a small window to take advantage of this approach. Be suitably humble and diplomatic. Others will have become desensitised anyway – and you will seem fresh. Be relevant and constructive. The worst mistake is to trash what other people have done before. Think of the past as a building block and be sensitive to the existing team's sense of pride in their work.

You, as the leader, will set the tone for the communications function and you can empower the team to deliver at a different level. Your arrival should signal the opportunity for change.

Before you arrive, take a good look at the company you are joining. Become hyper-conscious of what the company looks and sounds like from an external perspective. It is incredibly helpful to go in with a point of view and then test your hypothesis. Consider what will really shift the dial. Saturate yourself in the business and think big and holistically rather than sinking into the day-to-day minutiae. Don't go in with a scattergun approach.

Don't give in to your insecurities. But be aware of them.

Be a sponge and do a lot of listening. Put the hours in.

There is a tendency with some communications people to grandstand. Don't feel you have to boast about who you just had lunch with. Your team members won't be impressed; they will be rolling their eyes behind your back.

I am not a fan of the 'quick win' approach. It's more about an understanding of human collateral. I put a lot of time and energy into getting my team right. Look at the team – are they glass-half-full people? Will they block me? Are they up for it? Have I got the right mix of skills? Create a close team so that you have three musketeers who you can trust and confide in. If you are good and courageous you will be fronting up some difficult conversations, in all likelihood, with the senior leadership team. You will need allies – you can't do it on your own. You will need positive energy and good talent. The biggest risk is that you might be isolated.

"THE CEO LEFT A HAND-WRITTEN NOTE TO WELCOME ME. IT FELT AS IF I WAS WANTED."

ⓑ INSIGHTS

- Try to plan a start date that best suits the business – not the first day of results for example, or when everyone is away.
- Check with HR whether any member of the team wanted the job.
- Find out about the induction programme in advance.
- If there isn't one planned, take responsibility for your own on-boarding.
- Do as much research as you can possibly manage.
- If switching sectors, read all about your peer group of companies.
- Form your own views of the business.
- Try to take a break before you start.
- Find out who your PA will be or who will be your point of contact for computers, laptops, phones, IT passwords etc. Don't assume systems will be in place when you arrive.

For additional reading you may want to look at *The First 90 Days, Critical Success Strategies for New Leaders at all levels*, a generalist guide by Michael Watkins.

YOUR
APPROACH
FROM
DAY ONE

I find it helps having a nice big global crisis within your first 100 days. It is a fantastic way to meet everyone with daily and nightly global conference calls, and you make connections in fast real-time.

I believe in the value of seeing as many people as possible early on. All too soon life takes off and you get too bogged down in the day-to-day. Establish relationships with a variety of internal and external stakeholders. Thank God I did that early on – before the travel freeze was introduced.

Use your honeymoon period to suggest change – people will give you leeway.

People fall into the category of those who must achieve something in the first 100 days and those who prefer to get to know the lie of the land – the organisation and its relationships and politics – during that time. Whichever you are, make sure you are aligned with what the organisation expects. They might not have the same view as you.

I remember one CEO's perspective about what makes someone successful in their organisation. 'I can tell within the first 100 days if they are going to make it or not. If they're not, you'll see that people just stop communicating with them because they have not shown themselves to be fast enough at getting stuck in.' On the other hand, another CEO once told me, 'I can't stand people who give you the answer before you've finished giving them the question.' Getting this balance right is crucial during your first 100 days.

Don't try out your rudimentary Chinese on your new Chinese boss unless you are absolutely sure that what you think you are saying is what you are actually saying...

➜ I've always found it really useful for the first 100 days to keep a diary. Go back later, perhaps after six months, and look at your notes. In most instances your instincts will have been proved right.

➜ Be conscious that things that matter to the board, and what they perceive as important, may differ from your view. Pay attention to the board's concerns and be seen to address some of these – it will give you a licence to operate more widely and effectively.

➜ Go towards the sound of gunfire – don't dodge it.

➜ **For me your first month has to be about listening. The urge to opine on the state of the nation is great – but resist. You are allowed not to know everything.**

First impressions last. Make sure you manage your own image and reputation as carefully as the organisation's.

"I FIND IT HELPS HAVING A NICE BIG GLOBAL CRISIS; YOU MAKE CONNECTIONS IN FAST REAL-TIME."

No doubt one of the primary reasons former journalists are recruited into communications roles is their ability to spot a good tale, but I have had to adjust the terminology and reaction when one pops up. I quickly learned that looking sombre and uttering something like 'This could pose a serious reputational risk' is probably better than 'Jesus, that's a great story'.

For my first 100 days I followed your advice: first, listen; second, listen and third, listen again. I also made a point of taking notes of things that struck me as odd in the first three months. I was able to cross off about 80 per cent of these once I had settled in. However, I was able to use my fresh 'outsider's' perspective to improve the other 20 per cent.

In my first three months I had a project, which went straight to the CEO; I made absolutely sure this went well and I put everything into it.

Working in Switzerland, most people spoke English, but I made a point of always speaking to the assistants in French, as a courtesy.

Meet external advisers early on and establish your rules of engagement *very* early on.

Don't rush to judge. Give yourself time to get a good sense of people.

Put time in early with important contacts such as key journalists. Listen to their perspective.

Plan to make an impact quickly; do not rely on finding opportunities, but set out to make your own.

→ Ask dumb questions early on – you only get one chance – ideally in a protected environment during one-on-ones.

→ Talk to as many people as possible. Understand what the expectations are.
Tread gently and don't alienate.
Find who your allies are.
Bring in the fresh air.
Bring in the voice of reality.
Be the voice of the outside world.
Mean what you say.
Be authentic.

→ Be sure that you have a story to tell when you are introduced to people. Don't waste those five minutes with a banal 'hi'. It's like speed dating. Make a 60-second elevator-type pitch with key facts about your background, a mention of people you have in common (such as previous CEOs you might have worked with), and why you are relevant to them.

→ **The biggest mistake is to leap in; you need to understand the political realities. It can be a disaster if you rush in. Yes, there may well be things that you need to fix quickly but always bear in mind the longer game.**

Be confident. Trust yourself. Pick your moments to be upfront.

"ASK DUMB QUESTIONS EARLY ON."

YOUR APPROACH FROM DAY ONE

You will need friends. Even if you have been brought in to be the axe man or woman, you need allies. Try to find neutral advocates already in senior positions outside communications; people who will not necessarily benefit from your success or failure, but who are just wise heads. Find these people quickly – find out who can be trusted.

I know of two recent occasions where people have not worked out at their company because, with hindsight, they admit that they came in too aggressively. They picked out all that was wrong with the organisation and told everyone what needed to be changed, with no deference to past successes. It is more about listening first.

Make friends with the people who really make the place tick, from the PAs (*especially the PAs*) to IT support, receptionists, drivers and the post room.

The most important thing is energy. It's not about being crass and trying to oversell oneself with 'look at me', but having an intelligent approach to your own brand and managing perceptions about your ability and impact.

Make the most of those early meetings, as you may never get another chance for that kind of face time.

In your first couple of weeks, avoid coming between the Chairman and his opportunity to buy a painting he has had his eye on for years through your – albeit tangential – involvement in a monumental diary mix-up. Sotheby's trumps filming an internal video every time.

Build your profile. Don't stay in your office. Immerse yourself in the organisation. Listen and hover. Build rapport with colleagues; they will know where the pot-holes are.

My advice is, whatever you have gleaned from the media, the website, the commentariat – it will only ever give you a partial view; get out and meet your stakeholders or clients. This will use a serious amount of shoe leather. Hear their views. Hear their war stories. Only then will you really grasp the culture around the business.

Don't jump in too quickly with your strategy – you could find yourself in a real cul-de-sac.

"BUILD RAPPORT WITH COLLEAGUES; THEY WILL KNOW WHERE THE POT-HOLES ARE."

Test the team on what its key targets are – and be sure that they are aligned with your priorities.

The most critical thing is to understand the nature of the business and the need to speak with credibility. Understand and invest time in the business and get to know it. Don't bullshit. Spend the time and kick the tyres. Be sure you understand the nature of the business. What is the financial plan? Ask the CEO for his/her four priorities. Don't assume. They might not be obvious and need teasing out. Lock into those priorities. Don't come with waffle about aligning stakeholders; people will look at you as if you are from Mars. Be credible. Get into the business.

In big corporations, watch out – in tough times the wolves gather around the communications function. Don't let communications become an easy target; demonstrate that the function is integral and not a 'nice to have'. You are employed to enable it to be a better organisation.

Some big organisations are hugely political. Work out where the power lies, both with the existing leaders and with future leaders. You need to become bulletproof. You will need acute political antennae. Seek out the wise guide within the organisation – he or she will exist.

Rushing around everybody risks pleasing nobody.

Understand the key risks. They will vary according to the sector. What are the critical four or five risks that will have the potential to bring the company down? A crisis is not a risk. There will be work for you to do in defining risk. You are the communications person and need to be on the same page as everyone else.

Understand your budget. Make sure you are clear about what your budget will allow you to do. What do you add to the organisation? Don't play to suspicions that you are just an overhead.

Have you got the right quality people? You need a world cup team rather than journeymen.

Consider the big priorities of key audiences; keep focused.

Is this a company that takes reputation seriously? Is it prepared to be proactive? Be clear about what the expectations of the top execs are. Am I proactively driving a strategy or babysitting? This will determine the future. Your future.

Who are the third-party providers? Take a quick look at all of them – what are they costing? Are they the right organisations? Are they people I respect? Are they doing the right thing?

Know your business and know your function.

Before you join, gather all the written material you can lay your hands on. Wade through core statements, sustainability reports, everything.

Make sure that corporate affairs has got its own branding right. Make sure it isn't insecure or obscure.

By the end of 100 days you will need to have made an impression and your internal stakeholders should be glad to have you around.

In a global company, consider the most important centre for reputation management. Is it Brussels or Washington, DC? You might be surprised. Don't just be sure to have the right resources, make sure you have the right quality resources in the right place. There might be a critical country that you haven't considered.

ⓣ INSIGHTS

- Always take a notebook – write down first impressions and initial ideas in one place. You can refer back to this later and reflect on your instincts and what you have learned.
- Ask the same few key questions across various stakeholders to draw out the information you need.
- Take time to understand what is important to those who are important to you (those who will judge your success).
- Do one or two things sooner rather than later that are tangible (to those you have identified as your key stakeholders).
- Talk to your team on a one-to-one basis and as a group.
- Travel extensively across the business and across functions. Gather as much insight as possible.
- Establish your profile – be careful how you manage your brand.
- Ask dumb questions.
- Bring the outside in.
- Follow your instincts.
- Listen twice as much as you talk.
- Recognise you will have to live with the consequences if you rush your strategy.
- Do your due diligence on the perception and expectation of communications.
- Keep a perspective on stories of your 'old days'.
- Listen, reflect, act.

NAVIGATING THE POLITICAL AND CULTURAL LANDSCAPE

NAVIGATING THE POLITICAL AND CULTURAL LANDSCAPE

➡ Beware icebergs; every job has potential hazards. Listen very carefully to the subtext, particularly from advisers and major stakeholders.

➡ Never believe that your personal relationship with the CEO or other senior execs will be enough. Being at the top in communications can be a pretty friendless place – particularly when things are going wrong. If you understand where the support is on the ground, where the collaborators and the power bases are, you will be able to navigate through the tricky moments.

➡ You may join at a particular point of turmoil or tension. It can feel like a baptism of fire, but the upside is that you can earn your spurs quickly. In choppy waters, take the opportunity to show what you are made of.

➡ **Accept that you will not have heard all you need to know during the interview process – they were in sell mode, remember. Recognise that there might be quite a lot to uncover.**

I think I went into 'listening mode' and didn't give enough opinion. My MD told me that he had expected me to be more vocal: 'We hired you because of the experience you've got.'

Be careful about what you say to advisers. I clearly touched a nerve when I asked, 'How much is this account worth to you?'

Communications stands at the head of armed forces. You have to know what moves the troops and you have to know the business.

It can feel daunting starting a new job when you feel like the new kid in the playground with lots of hidden codes and histories to decipher. You need to work out the social dynamics pretty quickly. But watch your enthusiasm. By trying to fit in I felt compelled to say that I liked football and went as far as to name a club I liked. This just made matters worse. I mentioned Arsenal and they were all Chelsea fans...

I realised the culture was one which respected an authentic voice and so I decided not to pipe up at every meeting, but bide my time until I had something to say.

In my organisation you have to earn your spurs. I did this quite quickly and was seen as credible and a 'good guy'.

You can get caught in the crossfire of internal politics – but don't take anything too personally. While you might be getting a raw deal because of someone's bad mood, it might just be that they are having a bad day.

Build a network from the outset. Make a point of meeting people in other divisions and those that your own department mutters about negatively. And seek out people in areas where the communications team doesn't have good contacts.

"LISTEN VERY CAREFULLY TO THE SUBTEXT, PARTICULARLY FROM THE ADVISERS AND MAJOR STAKEHOLDERS."

Understand the governance dynamics: the relationship between the CEO and Chairman and their relationships with the board. Each might have different expectations. Don't ignore this – talk to them and agree what your role is.

It's all about listening. A good entry point, when gathering information and talking to any stakeholder is, 'What is the thinking behind x?'. It's a non-aggressive way to probe.

It is easy to stay in the C-suite, but you should get out and visit the divisions as soon as possible. I found that my team never left their desks – and produced stuff that was of no interest or relevance to the business.

Build a good relationship with the Chief Executive, Chairman and the non-execs. Do this by delivering for them – and not delegating seemingly trivial tasks to team members. If things are important enough for them to worry about, they're important enough for you to do.

As someone newly working in-house, my big learning has been to listen more and think much harder about what is being felt, but not voiced, by those around me. The barriers being described are so rarely the real blocks on the road.

Be aware of schoolyard relationships – look out for bullies and collaborators. Be careful which 'team' you side with or are perceived to be aligned with.

Establish your strategic priorities early and keep focused on these – don't let yourself be distracted.

As a new arrival, you have the perfect reason to ask questions – make the most of your legitimate curiosity.

Note down your initial impressions; these are often the most profound as they are uncluttered by the culture and history of the organisation.

If you are new to the industry, get to know it quickly – you are your organisation's senior corporate salesperson and the sooner you can speak on its behalf with confidence and credibility, the better.

Develop a strategic plan within 100 days and start delivering.

Go 'broad and deep' in terms of building relationships. Broad in terms of the wider business – to understand the company's products and services. Deep in terms of investing in personal relationships with key functions such as legal, risk, marketing, strategy. Get to know your peer group, because most decisions or actions will rely on their support or advice.

Find reasons to involve the business' managers in your agenda, and push them forward as spokespeople and advocates. They know more about the business than you. It will make your job easier, and they will help you build a network of supporters.

"IN CHOPPY
WATERS, TAKE
THE OPPORTUNITY
TO SHOW WHAT
YOU ARE MADE OF."

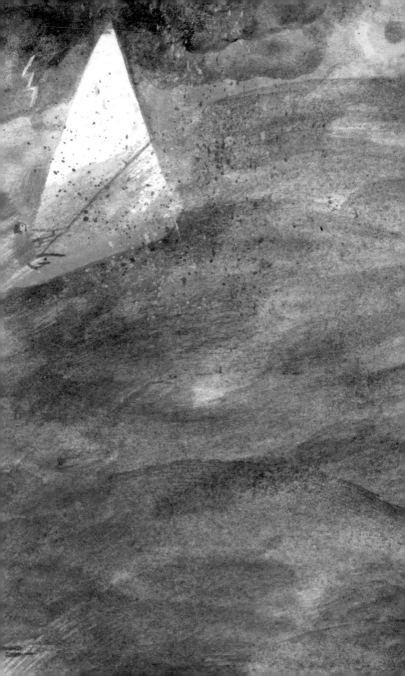

→ Be sensitive to the way people from different cultures like to get to know others. Westerners tend to go out for a drink and be quite casual. In my experience, the Chinese hate this, and prefer to have a big lunch and hear about your experience. I find that the Swiss like lots of formal meetings – ideally face-to-face – that always start on time and last for a set period. Video conferences can be disconnected on the hour, even if you are in mid-flow.

→ If you haven't had extensive experience handling a global function, it is a good idea to talk to those that have, before you start. There are some really useful tips and insights that can help you avoid some clangers. For example, I learned that if you don't follow up with Americans to confirm an action plan, they will tend to ignore you.

→ Moving from the UK to the US has thrown up some amusing linguistic challenges. I was very lucky to find a tongue-in-cheek guide to these early on. 'I hear what you say' for us Brits is a clear sign of disagreement and the end of the conversation, whereas here in the US it signals that you accept someone's point of view. Calling something a 'brave proposal' in the US is taken as genuine high praise – in the UK it's another way of saying, 'Are you crazy?' Finally, in America, suggesting to someone that they might consider other options doesn't send the intended clear message you don't like their idea, which it would in London. The lesson seems to be that us Brits never really say what we mean. Bear this in mind the next time someone doesn't understand your point.

→ **Get to know the CEO and other senior managers quickly – these are the crucial relationships for success.**

When people join a company, they need to focus less on the need to start delivering and instead to try to understand everything they possibly can about the business: what drives value, the competitive landscape, the business model. Too often people want to get straight into fixing tactical issues. It is important to have the broader context.

When you are new, make sure what you think you heard is what they said. Make notes at meetings and capture what you hear – and then bounce it off a trusted colleague. They will be able to help you get in tune and aligned, and you will feel confident that you haven't misinterpreted something. They will tell you what rings true and what doesn't.

Deliver something tangible early – this will establish your credentials and credibility.

Adapt to the language of the organisation; everyone has their own narrative. Mirror the language and behaviour of the top people and make sure you become part of the culture.

"IT CAN FEEL DAUNTING STARTING AT A NEW JOB. WORK OUT THE SOCIAL DYNAMICS PRETTY QUICKLY."

> It is important to come across as calm and thoughtful. I would rather be quiet and measured than big and shouty. You can always become shouty later, but best not at the beginning.

From my experience, the most important thing is to look and listen. There is nothing worse than a new person telling the organisation what is wrong on their first day. Get to understand the culture, the people, and find out about past successes as well as failures.

People will form an immediate opinion of you – that's why I try to be a 'blank canvas' for the first 30 days.

I think it is a good idea to fix a time with your CEO after the first 30 days and share your first impressions. A slightly more informal chat will work better than a presentation – it should be a discussion and a chance to build a rapport. This subtle and collaborative approach should be less confrontational too. But know your audience – only you can judge what will work best in the culture you have come into.

In the first week of my job I lost my temper with a journalist. I knew it was a mistake. Only lose your temper deliberately.

Keep smiling, don't communicate stress and never be seen running; it just makes people feel nervous and, really, what advantage is a few more seconds going to gain?

You are the brand ambassador and people are likely to read a lot into how you present yourself and what this says about the people or organisation you work for. I believe that politeness, charm and discretion are absolutely key. It is amazing what you can achieve with a smile and by being courteous.

Don't get heated and raise your voice. It is a sign that things are not going well and it will unsettle your team.

You are generally a keeper of a lot of secrets. I make it a rule not to share anything – that way I don't have to worry about what I have told to who.

"DON'T COMMUNICATE
STRESS AND NEVER
BE SEEN RUNNING;
IT JUST MAKES PEOPLE
FEEL NERVOUS."

ⓕ INSIGHTS

- Investigate legacy, governance and sources of power.
- Establish an internal network, including other new people.
- Involve the business managers.
- Proactively build relationships.
- Position yourself as part of the improvement cycle.
- Are you hearing what people are *really* saying? Double check.
- Assess the current attitudes towards the communications function. Is it taken seriously? Does it add value?
- Remind yourself of the complexities of working in a multi-national organisation and be very aware of cultural differences, potential *faux pas* and sensitivities.
- Consider cultural (internal and external) differences and the implications for your role.

Further reading such as *The EQ Edge, Emotional Intelligence and your Success* by Steven Stein might be useful.

TEAM
LEADERSHIP

"I TOLD THE TEAM MY DOOR WAS ALWAYS GOING TO BE OPEN.

I SET OUT A CLEAR LINE OF SIGHT AND TALKED OPENLY ABOUT MY VISION FOR THE FUNCTION."

Spend time with your team and get to know them. You need to show them what you're made of – and that you value them. They will see you through thick and thin if you do.

I work with a five-point plan:
- listen, research and audit carefully;
- engage, inspire and influence people early;
- plan your strategy thoughtfully;
- implement strongly;
- and finally, continually check the results and keep looking for ways to improve.

Recognise that your team will be looking for direction.

Understand and make understood your brand of leadership – and be consistent.

Remember that change will have been unsettling for your immediate team.

Demystify the corporate communications function. Don't over-complicate what you do.

You have been headhunted for good reason and people will want to see your direction and style. Be confident.

Try to engage everyone. Recognise the team, but include others and make the strategy relevant to everybody.

Recognise the workers – and keep an eye on those who just want to ingratiate themselves with you.

Carve out more than the induction time; get deep.

Be visible, show interest, make people know who you are.

Position yourself as part of the improvement cycle; position yourself as a strategic partner.

Having spent a lot of time with the organisation before my start date, gathering information and developing a lot of my strategy, day one was about being clear on the changes I wanted to make. There needed to be some symbolic act to show the need for urgent modernisation. I set out my strategy with an all-staff meeting where I told them that I had a track record of leading people through difficult times.

Team management and your own leadership style are critical elements of your likely success. I was used to leading teams in war zones. I know how important it is to be charismatic, even when you don't feel like it. Why should people follow you if you don't look as if you are committed?

Give yourself a deadline to make a difference and deliver something tangible. But make sure this is relevant to the team – and the company.

"GET RID OF POOR PERFORMERS QUICKLY. THEY ARE TOXIC AND THE REST OF THE TEAM WILL BE RELIEVED TO SEE YOU TAKING ACTION."

→ My predecessor had always had his door shut. I told the team that I wanted them to know that my door was always going to be open. I talked openly about my vision for the communications function – to make it central to the organisation and no longer siloed and out of touch. I made it clear that there were going to be five or six different tracks of change. It was a relatively high-risk strategy, but I knew I had to demonstrate a series of changes. People could have felt there was a tsunami of change and a risk that they might be overwhelmed, but I was very clear in my own communication and leadership style. In the first few months, you are very much aware of the importance of what you need to do, but also the potential fragility of your credibility.

→ Myers Briggs [tests to assess personality types] is rather helpful: if you know your preferred working style, and that of your boss and team members, you can anticipate tension areas and deal with them.

→ Articulate a clear sense of direction for the communications function. Separate 'business as usual' and reactive work from proactive work that will make a difference to reputation. Write it down on a single page of A4 and keep it with you so you can repeat it.

→ Whilst you are likely to need to be seen to make some changes with your team, don't throw the baby out with the bath water. You might find that some people just haven't been given a chance to shine before and, under new direction, quickly thrive and go on to do very well.

→ **Motivate your team and remember, they will be your biggest supporters if you do well – and your biggest critics if you don't.**

Focus on relationships in the first few months; use the opportunity of being new to build relationships. I would focus a lot on the team. I do feel that if I had my time again, I would build better bonds with the team on arrival and be more sensitive to what my arrival meant to them. I'm a nice guy and I assumed everyone would 'get' that, but of course they were all preoccupied with their own job security and the threat of change.

As a Communications Director, a key lesson for me has been the importance of making sure people know when they are doing a good job.

I wanted to inject energy into the team and so introduced a short, daily, stand-up information briefing session for the whole team, to keep them informed and provide a chance to share ideas.

I try to have one-to-ones with each member of the team and then I can triangulate what they say and find out what is working well. It also helps you get a sense of the dynamics of the team. By setting up an intensive round of meetings with key stakeholders internally and externally, you are soon able to gain a strong sense of what the problems and opportunities are. In one case it became very clear that the team thought everything was going well – but all the stakeholders thought the communications function was crap.

When someone says quietly, 'Your team will need some attention' you know it's a basket case. Get rid of poor performers quickly. They are toxic and the rest of the team will be relieved to see you taking action. Set out your style and vision. You need your troops behind you.

"WHAT GOES AROUND
COMES AROUND.
TAKE CARE OF YOUR
RELATIONSHIPS
AND YOUR
PERSONAL BRAND."

Make the princes your friends, as well as the king.

Take every single member of your team – and contractors – aside for an hour and say, 'Tell me three things that must change and three things we should not change'. You will gather some really useful data. I knew by the end of day two who was going to make it in my team and who was not. I looked into the eyes of a third of my team and all I saw was the back of their skull. They were not going to be the ones wanted for the voyage.

Make a point of getting to know the support people – they can make your life really tedious if you don't get them on-side. Find out who your contacts are for IT and HR in particular and explain what you are looking to them for, and ask what works for them in terms of ensuring a strong business partnership.

Fix your relationships with HQ before you go out to the operating companies – probably by month two – and talk to the regional CEOs and those in their communications function. I follow the money and start with the biggest markets and work down, according to their P&L.

Ask your peers and those to whom you report, 'Tell me one thing that in a year from now will show that I have made a difference'.

By the end of the first month, you can start conveying your findings and addressing your strategy. You will have spoken to the execs (half the board probably), all the global function leaders, and the team, and will have the 'three things' feedback to work on and know 'what good looks like'.

My key tip is, 'What goes around comes around'. Take care of your relationships and your personal brand.

In your first month, bring in all the suppliers and tell them, 'I need to understand what you do for us'. You will be astonished how many suppliers can't answer this simple request. It can be an effective way to terminate unnecessary contracts.

℞ INSIGHTS

- Spend time with your team; talk on a one-to-one basis and as a group. Find out what matters to them.
- Set out your leadership style and your vision quickly.
- Identify the weak performers as soon as possible and decide how you are going to manage them.
- Identify true collaborators.
- Put the hours in and lead by example.

Leadership is likely to be one of the most critical elements of your early days. How you connect with your team, manage your own profile, manage key relationships and set direction can all make a big difference to your success. One of the recurring themes is about the need to be yourself and be authentic, but recognise when to be flexible.

Further reading that you might want to consider includes *Why Should Anyone Be Led You* by Rob Goffee and Gareth Jones, *The Wisdom of Teams* by Jon R Katzenbach and Douglas K Smith and *The Five Dysfunctions of a Team* by Patrick Lencioni.

AFTER THE
FIRST MONTH

→ Choose a suitable time to present your initial findings and proposals to the board – your opportunity to say, 'This is what I am finding strange, this is what we need to do, these are some solutions, this is the commitment I need from you'.

→ Unless you deal with negativity, you can forget any chance of building positivity.

→ Pay attention to the longer game. See the strategic dimension going forward.

→ Keep alert to the need to preserve objectivity and your external orientation. And never forget the importance of keeping a network.

→ **As you get settled, have a portfolio of initiatives that will have impact over different timeframes – in other words, have a mix of deliverables in your sightline.**

Make sure you fully and precisely understand the issues and challenges you are being asked to address before proposing solutions – unless you want to find yourself answering entirely the wrong questions.

→ I have learned that most 'vision' is *how* you communicate, rather than the detail; it doesn't need over-refinement.

→ While your background is interesting and there will be value in referring back to it to help establish your credibility, there is a limit to how much you should talk about your old companies. Don't jabber on and on about how great your previous jobs were.

→ Making connections and meeting people across the business can be done in a number of ways, but I found a really great opportunity to do that was by joining the volunteer programme. We had a beach-cleaning project one weekend with a picnic, for example, and it gave me the chance to meet a cross-section of people I would never normally meet. I also joined the company business university's weekly 'lunch & learn' programme, where all sorts of topics across the business were discussed and explained. Making time for those things was very useful.

→ Relaunching the intranet is never the answer to institutional internal communications problems.

→ **I do think that if I did it all again, I would come out earlier with a vision. There were forces preventing me from doing that, but nonetheless, now I would push forward and involve the team.**

"RE-LAUNCHING THE INTRANET IS NEVER THE ANSWER TO INSTITUTIONAL INTERNAL COMMUNICATION PROBLEMS."

Other new people can make great allies – make sure you connect. Support them, and they'll do the same for you.

Listen and question in your first month, but also spot a couple of symbolic things to get on with that are low risk, low cost, and set the tone. You want to be decisive without rushing into something you'll later want to unpick. For my part, I always try to identify an early cost saving to knock down the 'comms people don't know the real value of money' preconception. I also try to do something involving talent and development, to demonstrate a desire to invest in people, and build goodwill and trust for when you ask people to do things differently. Spend lots of time with your team and getting to know the business; build your knowledge and your mandate. Decide the areas you're going to focus on first, and then go in deep. This includes key relationships with journalists.

In the second month, start to lay out some of your ideas and begin to test them to see whether you're on the right track. You've got a great window to challenge and bring in new thinking, but you will want to 'socialise' your ideas and get buy-in so you don't shock the organisation later on – or miss something because you don't have the full picture. Build your plans in a way which integrates the pre-existing business strategy and ways of framing it – rather than reinventing the wheel.

Always do at least one non-urgent thing a day.

In the third month, begin to implement some bigger changes, focusing on what will deliver in the medium term. Hopefully by this point you will have built a sense of ownership in your ideas and have a degree of consensus and buy-in.

I like to do a mini strategic review, to get the team plan on a page and everyone lined up behind it. This can be revisited at the half-year mark so it doesn't need to be set in stone, but creates a framework.

Hand out plenty of praise.

Build relationships – make the effort to get to know people and their interests, rather than just focus on the functional completion of tasks. Socialise, because you will often get the real story over a glass of wine.

Figure out the shadow organisation – not just the org that's laid out on the org chart. Work out who knows and likes whom, who has history, insight, ideas...

Avoid frightening your peers – it can be easy to come across as empire building or threatening. Focus on supporting and learning in those early weeks and months.

Don't hide behind e-mail – get out and about. You'll always get more from a proper conversation.

℞ INSIGHTS

- Share ideas, priorities and expectations with the team, the senior management and with your peer group.
- Start to develop a draft plan.
- Draw up plans in detail.
- Start to implement them.
- Avoid jabbering about your old job.
- Be aware of your profile, perceptions and your leadership style.
- Accept that you may have to flex your style or adjust your expectations on timeframes.

Some additional reading that might be useful includes *Practice what you Preach* by David Maister, *18 Challenges of Leadership* by Trevor Waldock & Shenaz Kelly-Rawat, and *Quiet Leadership* by David Rock.

BY THE END
OF 100 DAYS

"LISTEN CAREFULLY."

If you are asked to make a presentation, it's not always a good idea to work alone. We had a problem with a regional head of communications who was determined to research and write his own presentation, with no sense-check with the group. He wanted ownership, and in spite of the fact that I advised very strongly that he needed to be sure that we were all aligned, he went ahead. The problem was that half of what he said was just plain wrong, and the CEO had to correct him, in front of the rest of the board. It was embarrassing. He lost their confidence and his credibility never recovered.

Don't forget why they brought you in.

Your instincts are always right. In some cases I was persuaded to change my mind, but actually all my first thoughts and impressions were correct. Don't let your judgement be clouded by other people trying to influence you.

There is no substitute for an evidence-based analysis when presenting to the senior leadership team. Your hand is stronger if you have solid evidence and something tangible. The modern Communications Director has to move to something firmer than gut feel.

Accept that you will be a complete dork at some time or other. My top tip would be to double check who is being put through to you, so that you can deal with the call appropriately. I took a call where I assumed it was a friend messing about. It wasn't the greatest career moment to find that I had just said 'get stuffed' to the Chairman of Deutsche Bank...

Be a listener. Try to understand what was working and people's priorities – and build a mandate for change. I deliberately came in at Q1 so that I could make my strategy presentation in line with the calendar timetable – linking the two to get a mandate for change. It was absolutely critical that there was a change in approach to communications and a need to build a consistent narrative.

Don't neglect old contacts – and keep up the networking.

"I DON'T RECOMMEND COMING IN AND TELLING THE BOARD THAT THEIR WORK HAS ALL BEEN AWFUL AND YOU ARE, EFFECTIVELY, THE NEW MESSIAH."

Be sensitive to the culture.

Be sure to listen to external advisers; gather up as much information as possible.

Align initiatives so that your plans are thought through and consistent.

Never assume; listen.

Give credit for work that merits credit.

Be very careful about how to talk about change; you need to be wary of expectations and the timeframe.

I don't recommend coming in and telling the board that their work has all been awful and that you are, effectively, the new messiah. That is something I have witnessed, and saw that it only isolated the individual concerned.

You have to work out where your mandate is, and who your patrons are.

Where is your licence to operate?

Align your brand of leadership with the existing management structure.

Be bold. I took a completely fresh approach to how the results were going to be presented and found a new venue. Huge pictures, stories, the journey, a multimedia approach... it had big impact and created a massive shift in perception about how communications could help the business.

▣ INSIGHTS

- Familiarisation should be complete.
- Your vision and goals are communicated.
- Your network internally has solid foundations.
- Pick up with mentors and advisers to make sure you keep your clarity of vision and sense of perspective.

Looking ahead...

- Keep on top of your own development programme and/or conference speaker opportunities.
- Keep, and date, regular notes (in a single place such as a small note book) of your team members' successes and any particular problem or incidents. This makes the annual appraisal so much easier and you come across as being more credible if you can be specific.
- Reflect at the end of each week if anyone in the team could do with a short email or personal 'thank you'.
- Plan and book in the diary a date for a six-monthly review with your own line manager.
- Consider using a coach for objective and insightful guidance.

"YOU WILL NEED YOUR ALLIES. YOU CAN'T DO IT ON YOUR OWN. YOU NEED POSITIVE ENERGY AND GOOD TALENT."

YOU SHOULD
ENJOY YOUR JOB
AND HAVE FUN.

THERE ARE DAYS
WHEN THINGS DO
NOT GO SO WELL
AND YOU WAKE UP
AT 3AM, BUT YOU
HAVE TO KEEP YOUR
FOCUS ON LONG-TERM
GOALS AND YOU
SHOULD HAVE THE
COURAGE OF YOUR
CONVICTIONS.

CONTRIBUTORS

 Paul Abrahams
Duncan Bonfield
Andrew Brown
Stuart Bruseth
Jonathan Charles
Dominic Cheetham
Paul Clarke
Tim Cobb
Alex Cole
Andraea Dawson Shepherd
Sue Garrard
Emma Gilpin Jacobs
Jenny Grey
Clare Harbord
Paddy Harverson
Jeremy Hillman
Chris Hogg
Howell James
Sian Jarvis
Steve John
Charlotte Lambkin
Simon Lewis
Andrew Moys
Paul Mylrea
Charles Naylor
Sally Osman
Stephen Pain
Matt Peacock
John Shield
Michael Stewart
Brigitte Trafford
Chris Wade
Mark Ware

The contributors have been most generous with their time and their willingness to share their experience, for which we thank them most sincerely.

Designed & produced by Red Giant / rglondon.co.uk

NOTES